CLASSIC PIANO REPERTOIRE

CHRISTMAS

12 SEASONAL FAVORITES

ARRANGED FOR SOLO PIANO

BY EDNA MAE BURNAM, WILLIAM GILLOCK,

GLENDA AUSTIN, CAROLYN C. SETLIFF,

MELODY BOBER, AND MORE!

ISBN 978-1-4803-5043-4

WILLIS MUSIC

EXCLUSIVELY DISTRIBUTED BY

HAL•LEONARD®

Visit Hal Leonard Online at
www.halleonard.com

CLASSIC PIANO REPERTOIRE

FROM THE PUBLISHERS

The *Classic Piano Repertoire* series includes popular as well as lesser-known pieces from a select group of composers out of the Willis piano archives (established in 1899). This special Christmas volume features 12 great seasonal arrangements by several Willis composers, ranging from early intermediate to advanced. Each piece has been newly engraved and edited for this compilation.

CONTENTS

The First Noël

for Donna Boyd

Traditional 18th Century French Melody
Arranged by Glenda Austin

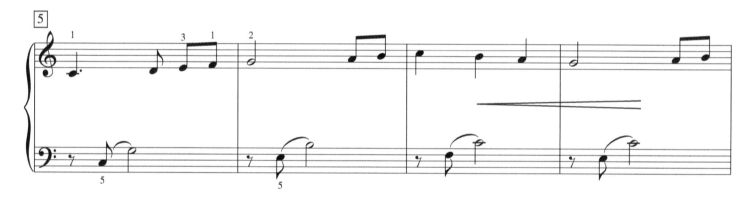

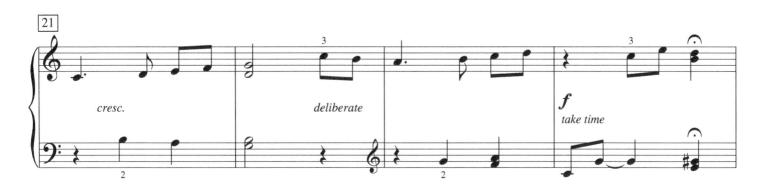

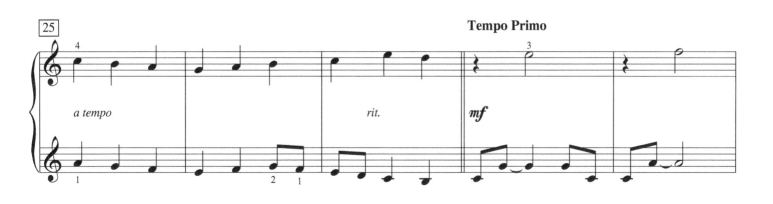

Go, Tell It on the Mountain

Traditional
Arranged by Glenda Austin

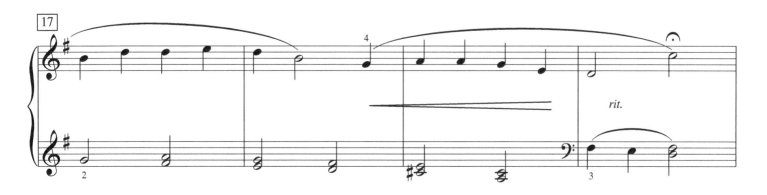

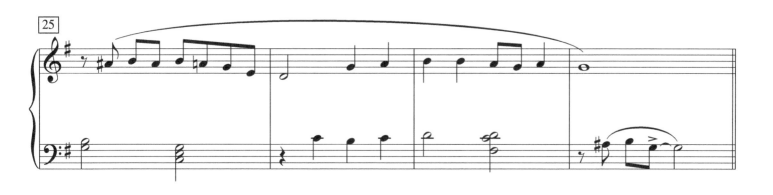

Shepherds, Shake Off Your Drowsy Sleep!

Traditional French Carol
Arranged by Katherine Beard

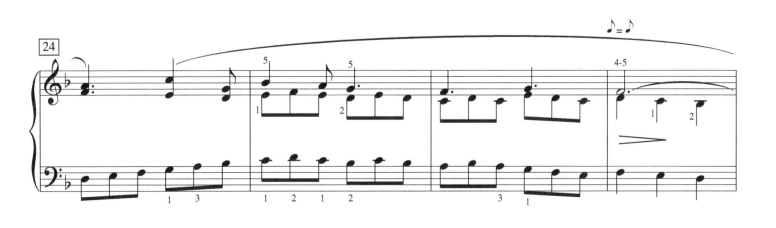

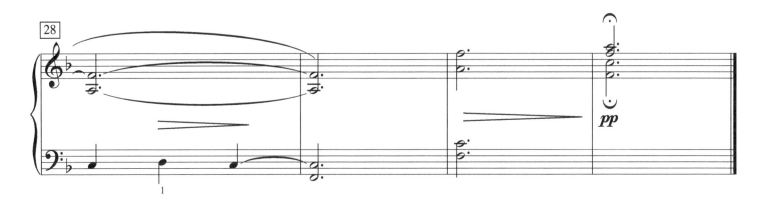

What Child Is This?
(Greensleeves)

English Folk Song
Arranged by Edna Mae Burnam

O Come, All Ye Faithful

By J. Reading
Arranged by Carolyn Miller

The Holly and the Ivy

18th Century English Carol
Arranged by Katherine Beard

Toyland
from BABES IN TOYLAND

Words by Glen MacDonough
Music by Victor Herbert
Arranged by William Gillock

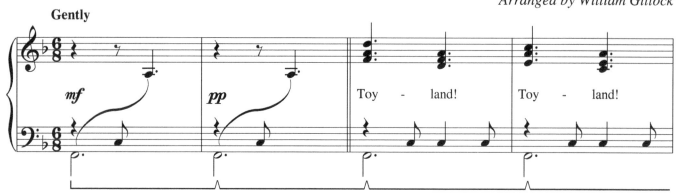

ne'er _ re - turn a - gain.

O Come, O Come Emmanuel

Gregorian, 8th Century
Arranged by Carolyn C. Setliff

(With light pedal)

Sing We Now of Christmas

French Carol
Arranged by Carolyn C. Setliff

To Chris, Mona, Katy, Billy, Matt and Nicky

March of the Toys

By Victor Herbert
Arranged for piano solo by Edna Mae Burnam

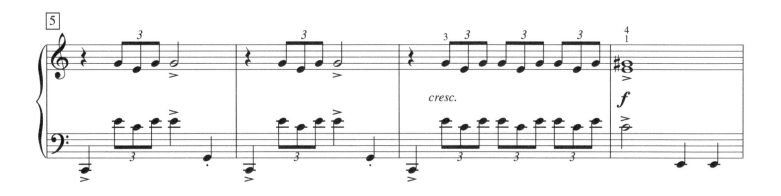

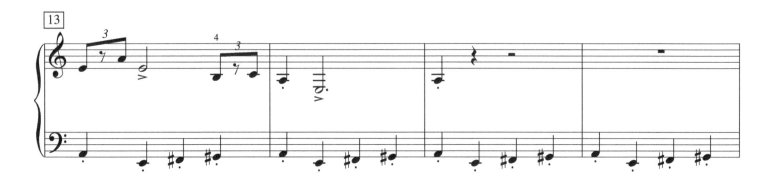

2nd time to Coda ⊕

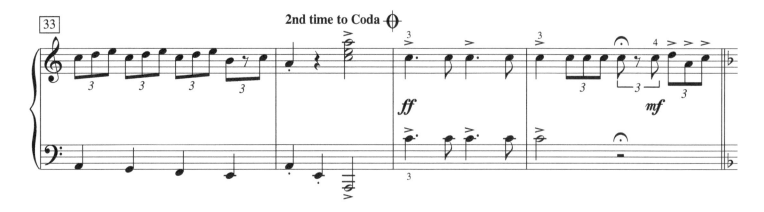

D.C. al Coda

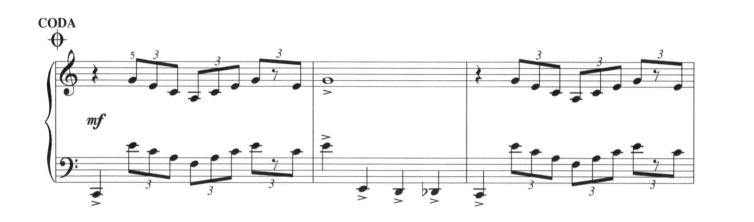

Silent Night

Franz Gruber
Arranged by Melody Bober

God Rest Ye Merry, Gentlemen

Traditional
Arranged by Melody Bober

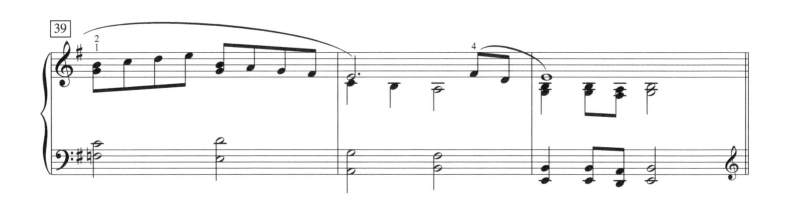

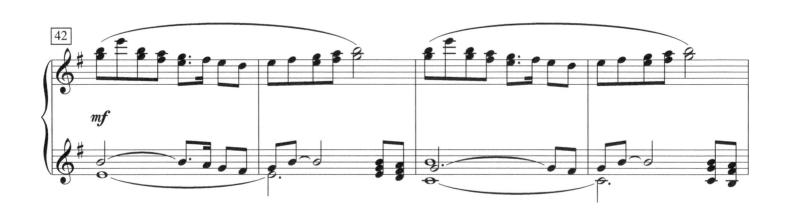

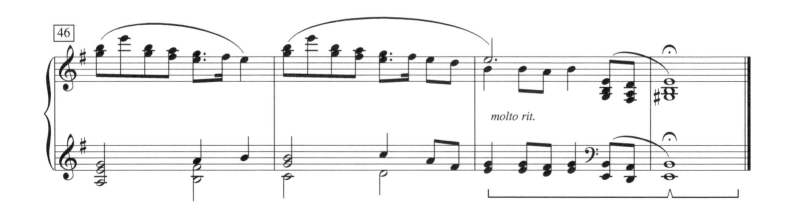